SRA

Imagine It!

Skills Practice

Workbook

Level K
Book 2

McGraw Hill SRA

Columbus, OH

SRAonline.com

SRA

An Open Court Curriculum.

Printed in the United States of America.

Send all inquiries to this address:
SRA/McGraw-Hill
4400 Easton Commons
Columbus, OH 43219-6188

ISBN: 978-0-07-610473-4
MHID: 0-07-610473-7

7 8 9 WCE 13 12 11 10

The McGraw-Hill Companies

Table of Contents

Unit 6 My Shadow

Unit 7 Teamwork

Unit 8 Ready, Set, Grow!

Unit 9 Red, White, and Blue

Unit 10 Windy Days

Name ______________________ **Date** ________

Jj

J

j

Directions: Write the capital and small forms of the letter *Jj*. Write the letter *j* under the picture whose name begins with the /j/ sound.

Name ______________________ **Date** __________

Directions: Write the letter *j* under each picture whose name begins with the /j/ sound.

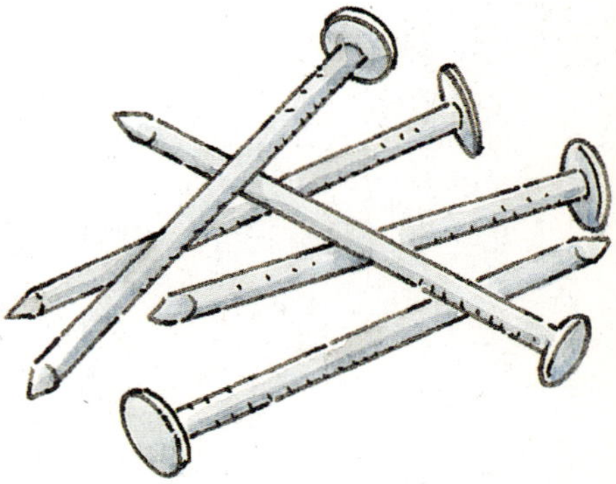

Name ______________________________ **Date** __________

Directions: Listen carefully as I read the paragraph. Put a slash where a space should appear in the paragraph.

I went to the park.I stood by a tree.It was sunset.The sun made shadows for the tree and me.Our shadows were very tall.The tree was taller than I was.

Name ______________________ Date __________

Directions: Write the capital and small forms of the letter *Ff*.
Write the letter *f* under the picture whose name begins with the /f/ sound.

Ff

F

f

Name ______________________ **Date** __________

Directions: Write the letter *f* under each picture whose name begins with the /f/ sound.

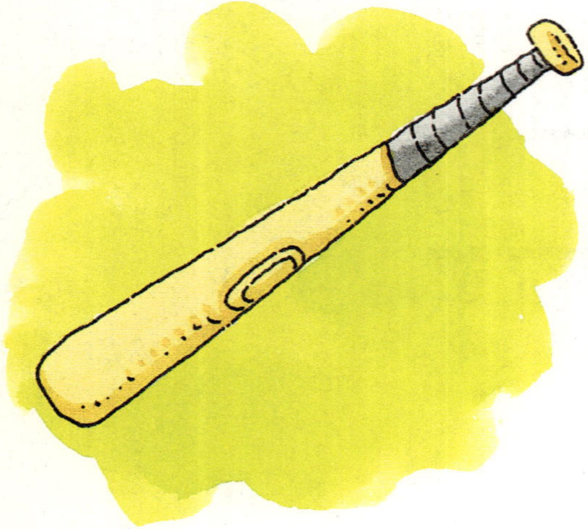

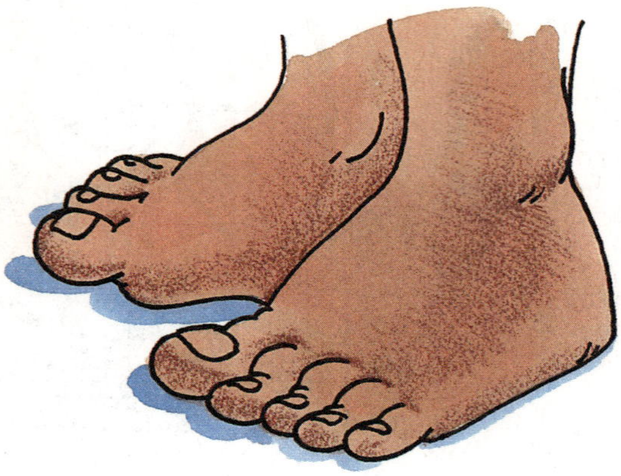

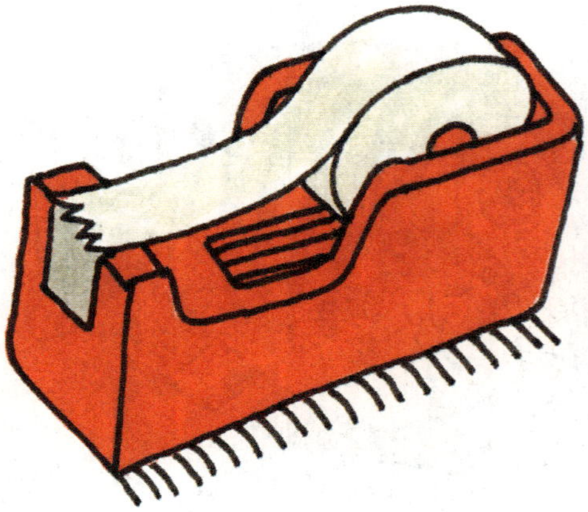

Name ______________________ **Date** ________

Directions: Circle the objects in the pictures whose names begin with the /f/ sound. Write the capital form of the letter *Ff* on the line.

F

Name ______________________ Date __________

Directions: Listen as I read the sentences. Circle the sentence in the right column that has a different beginning.

1.	I see the dog.	I see the dog's brown hair. The dog has brown hair.
2.	Here is my lunch.	I am eating a sandwich. Here is my sandwich.
3.	He drew a picture.	His picture is of a monkey. He drew a monkey.
4.	He plays soccer.	He plays soccer very well. She is a great soccer player!

Name ______________________ **Date** __________

Directions: Circle the word with the beginning /j/ or /f/ sound that names the picture. Then write the letter on each line that makes the /j/ or /f/ sound.

fan tan

pump jump

hot jam

Name ______________________ Date ________

Directions: Circle the pictures whose names end with the /f/ sound. Write the small form of the letter *Ff* on the line.

f

Name ______________________ **Date** ________

Directions: Write the capital and small forms of the letter *Uu*. Write the letter *u* under the picture whose name has the /u/ sound.

Uu

U

u

Name ______________________ **Date** __________

Directions: Write the letter *u* under each picture whose name has the /u/ sound.

Name ______________________ **Date** ________

Directions: Write the capital and small forms of the letter *Xx*. Write the letter *x* under the picture whose name ends with the /ks/ sound.

Xx

X

x

Name ______________________ **Date** __________

Directions: Write the letter x under each picture whose name ends with the /ks/ sound.

Name ______________________ **Date** ________

Directions: Write the capital and small forms of the letter Zz. Write the letter z under the picture whose name begins with the /z/ sound.

Zz

Z

z

Name ______________________ **Date** ________

Directions: Write the letter z under each picture whose name begins with the /z/ sound.

Name ______________________ Date __________

Directions: Say each picture name. Circle the letter in the name that makes the /z/ sound.

rose

eggs

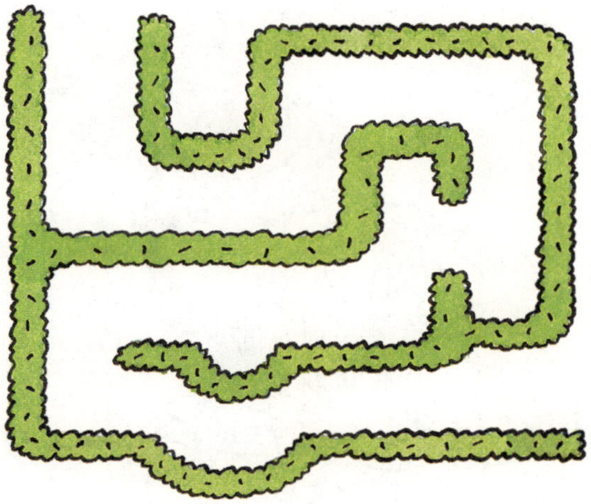

maze

buzz

Name ______________________ **Date** ________

Directions: Say each picture name. Circle the letter in the name that makes the /z/ sound.

prize

nose

fuzz

wigs

Name ______________________ Date __________

Directions: Name each picture. Write the letter *j* if the name begins with the /j/ sound. Write the letter *f* if the name begins with the /f/ sound. Write the letter *u* if you hear the /u/ sound.

Name ______________________ Date __________

Directions: Listen as I say the name for each picture. Write the missing letter on the line.

_an

b_g

_ox

_ar

Name ______________________ Date __________

Directions: Listen as I say the name for each picture. Write the missing letter on the line.

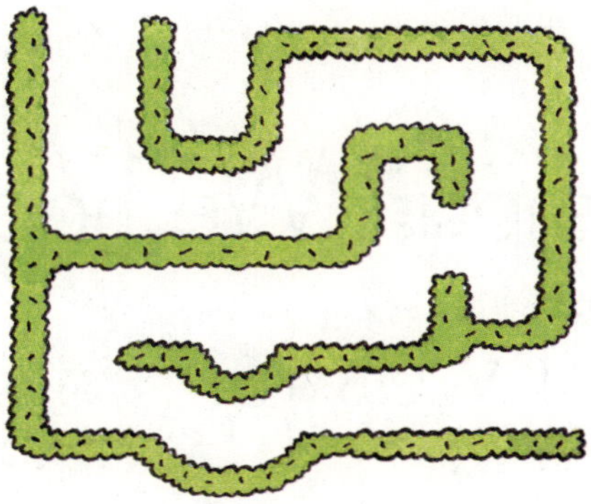

ma e

m g

ork

ebra

bo

acket

Name ______________________ **Date** __________

Directions: Listen carefully as I read the paragraph. Put a slash where a space should appear in the paragraph.

One day, we went to the park.We had a picnic and played games.It was fun. Then there was a storm.It had lightning and thunder.We went home.

Name ______________________ **Date** ________

Directions: Write the capital and small forms of the letter *Ww*. Write the letter *w* under the picture whose name begins with the /w/ sound.

Ww

W

w

Name ______________________ **Date** ________

Directions: Write the letter w under each picture whose name begins with the /w/ sound.

Name ______________________ Date __________

Directions: Listen carefully to what I say. Circle the correct picture.

1.

2.

3.

4.

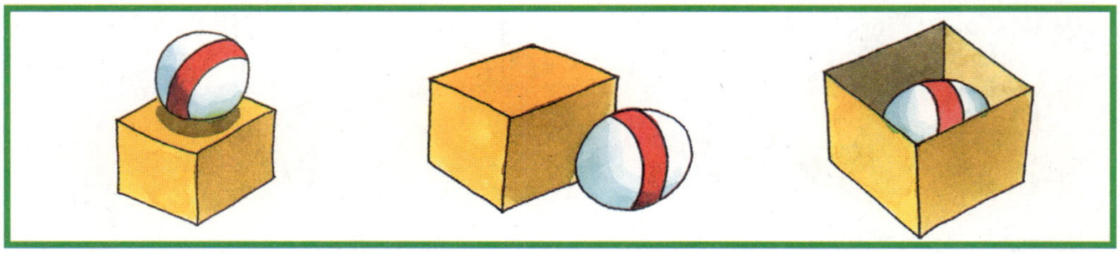

5.

Name ______________________ Date __________

Directions: Listen carefully to what I say. Circle the correct word.

6.  between in front of

7.  in over

8.  under on

9.  beside between

10.  under above

Name ______________________ Date __________

Directions: Write the capital and small forms of the letter *Kk*. Write the letter *k* under the picture whose name begins with the /k/ sound.

Kk

K

k

Name ________________ **Date** ________

Directions: Write the letter *k* under each picture whose name begins with the /k/ sound.

Name ______________________ **Date** __________

Letter

Draw a picture of the person receiving your letter.

To ______________________

Directions: Draw a picture of the person who will receive the class letter.

Name ______________________ Date __________

Letter Draw a picture of something the person receiving your letter likes or likes to do.

Directions: Draw a picture of something the person receiving your letter likes or likes to do.

Name ______________________ **Date** __________

Directions: Look at the pictures. Put them in order using the numbers *1*, *2*, and *3*.

Name ______________________________ Date __________

Directions: Draw a line from the picture to the word in the order that they happen.

First

Next

Last

Name ______________________ Date __________

Directions: Circle the word with the /w/ or /k/ sound that names each picture. Then write the letter on each line that makes the /w/ or /k/ sound.

web bed

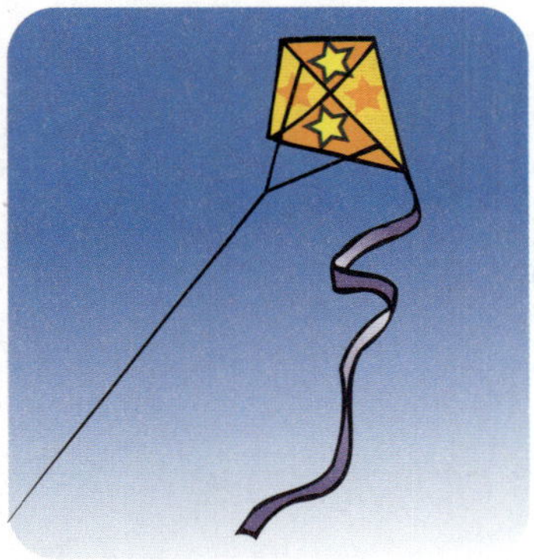

kite bike

yes keys

Name ______________________ Date __________

Directions: Circle the word with the /w/ or /k/ sound that names each picture. Then write the letter on each line that makes the /w/ or /k/ sound.

ring king

wig pig

bag wags

Name ______________________________ Date __________

Directions: Listen carefully to the words I read. Circle the position word.

1.	where	under	however
2.	behind	why	because
3.	who	until	inside
4.	first	on	next
5.	between	since	what
6.	how	so	over

Name ______________________________ **Date** __________

Directions: Look at the pictures and listen to the sentences I read. Circle the position word in each sentence.

7. A squirrel sits on a log.

8. The cat walks between the bowls.

9. A mouse hides in the paper.

10. The bird is over the worm.

Name ______________________ **Date** ________

Directions: Write the capital and small forms of the letter *Ee*. Write the letter e under the picture whose name has the /e/ sound.

Ee

E

e

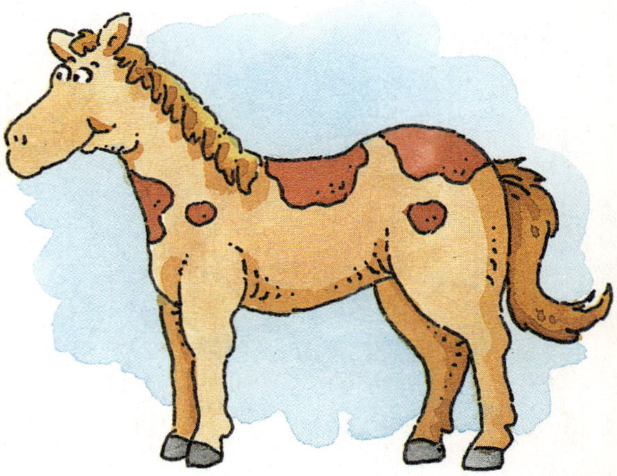

Name ______________________ **Date** ________

Directions: Write the letter e under each picture whose name has the /e/ sound.

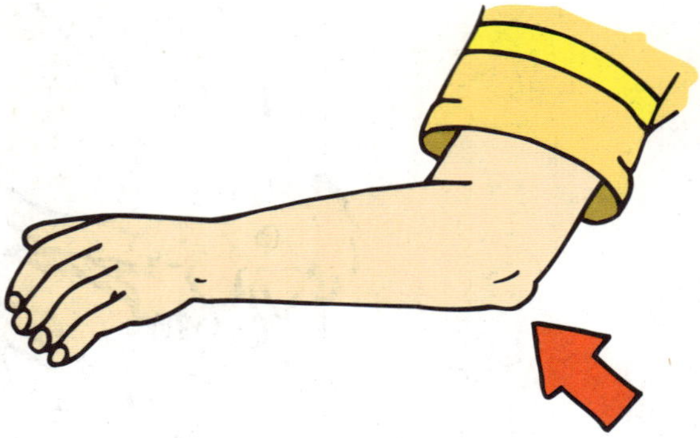

Name ______________________ Date __________

Directions: Write the capital and small forms of the letter *Qq*. Write the letter *q* under the picture whose name begins with the /kw/ sound.

Qq

Q

q

Name ______________________ Date __________

Directions: Write the letter q under each picture whose name begins with the /kw/ sound.

Name ______________________ Date __________

Directions: Listen carefully as I read each sentence. Circle the pronoun *I* or *You* in each sentence.

1. I like to run.

2. You are the teacher.

3. You love to play soccer.

4. I am happy.

5. I like oranges.

6. You have brown hair.

7. You have a dog.

8. I read a book.

Name ______________________ **Date** __________

Directions: Listen carefully as I read each sentence and the two words. Circle the word that replaces *I* or *You* in the sentence.

9. You can paint the fence.

ball Brenda

10. I will ride a bus to school.

Chris baseball

11. You can swim.

wagon Andrea

12. I saw the giraffes.

Henry apple

Name ______________________ **Date** __________

Directions: Write the capital and small forms of the letter *Yy*. Write the letter *y* under the picture whose name begins with the /y/ sound.

Yy

Y

y

Name ______________________ **Date** ________

Directions: Write the letter *y* under each picture whose name begins with the /y/ sound.

Name ______________________ **Date** __________

Directions: Write the capital and small forms of the letter *Vv*. Write the letter *v* under the picture whose name begins with the /v/ sound.

Vv

V

v

Name ______________________ Date __________

Directions: Write the letter v under each picture whose name begins with the /v/ sound.

Name ______________________________ **Date** __________

Directions: Listen carefully as I read each sentence. Underline the word that should be capitalized.

1. Dillon and i rode a horse.

2. i love to swim!

3. Jacob said, "i am hungry!"

4. Abby and i play checkers.

5. i ride the bus to school.

Name ______________________ **Date** __________

Directions: Listen carefully as I read each sentence. Fill in the shorter line with the pronoun I. Remember to capitalize I. Write another word on the longer line to complete the sentence.

1. ______ am __________ years old.

2. ______ have __________ hair.

3. My friend and ______ like to __________.

4. ______ have __________ eyes.

5. ______ have __________ pets.

Name ______________________ **Date** __________

Directions: Circle the word that names the picutre. Then write the letter on each line that makes the /w/ or /k/ sound.

wagon bag

king sing

wave move

Name ____________________ **Date** ________

Directions: Write the letter e under each picture whose name has the /e/ sound.

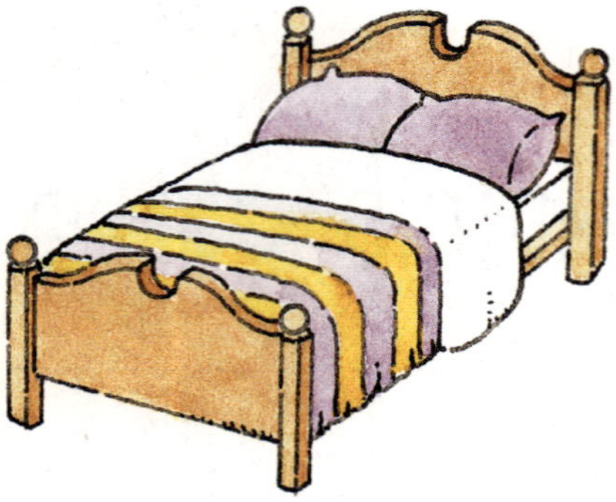

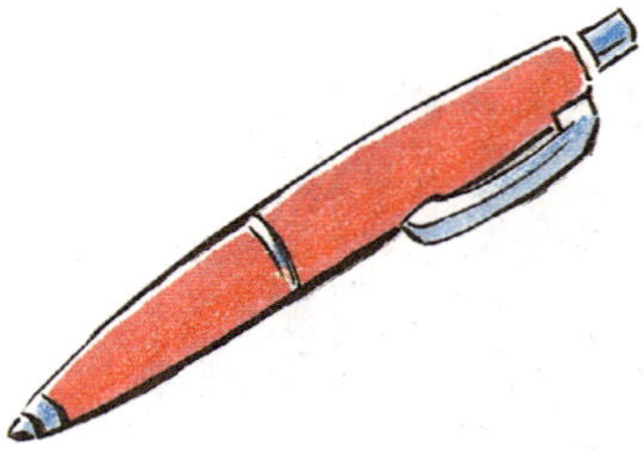

Name ______________________ **Date** __________

Directions: Write the capital and small forms of the letter *Aa*. Write the letter *a* under the picture whose name has the /ā/ sound.

Aa

Aa

A

a

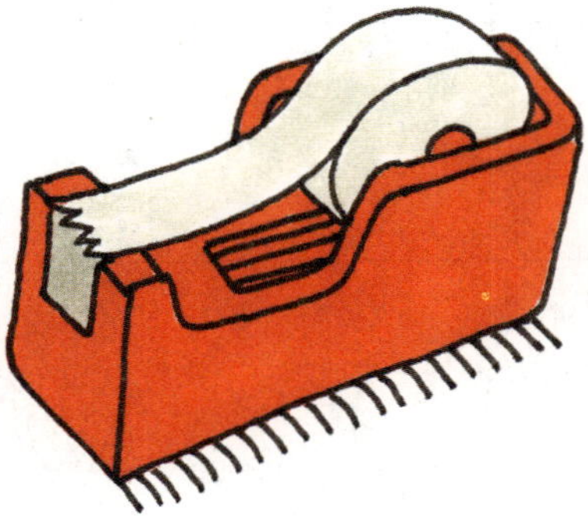

Name ______________________ **Date** __________

Zero 0

Directions: Trace the *0*s on the first line. Write a row of *0*s on the second line. Trace the word *zero* on the third line. Practice writing the word *zero* on the fourth line.

0 0 0 0 0 0

zero zero zero zero

Name ______________________ **Date** __________

Directions: Listen carefully as I read each sentence. Circle the pronoun that replaces the underlined word.

1. <u>Mr. Jones</u> drives a truck.

   It She He

2. <u>The airplane</u> flies.

   It She He

3. <u>Maria</u> is at the playground.

   It She He

4. <u>Alex</u> runs fast.

   It She He

5. <u>The castle</u> was big.

   It She He

6. <u>Mrs. Carter</u> loves to teach.

   It She He

Name ______________________ **Date** __________

Directions: Write the letter *a* under each picture whose name has the /ā/ sound.

Name ______________________ **Date** ________

One 1

Directions: Trace the *1s* on the first line. Write a row of *1s* on the second line. Trace the word *one* on the third line. Practice writing the word *one* on the fourth line.

1 1 1 1 1 1 1 1 1 1

one one one one one

Name ________________________ **Date** ________

Directions: Listen carefully as I read each sentence and the answers. Circle the pronoun that replaces the underlined words.

1. Lauren, Kristen, and Mel went to the store.

   We They

2. Meg and Tara eat lunch.

   We They

3. Sandy and I jump rope.

   We They

4. Bill and Pedro read books.

   We They

5. Grandpa and I play games.

   We They

6. My brother, Aunt Kelly, and I ride bikes.

   We They

Name ______________________ **Date** __________

Directions: Write the numbers *0* and *1* on the lines. Count the number of apples in each tree and write the correct number on the line.

0

1

Name ______________________ **Date** ________

Directions: Listen carefully as I read each sentence and the answers. Circle the pronoun that replaces the underlined words.

1. Jacob walked home.

   He it

2. Ashley read the book.

   She it

3. Anthony and I have brown hair.

   We They

4. The dog and cat are napping.

   We They

5. Jeff writes a letter.

   He She

6. Kelly and I jump rope.

   We They

Name ______________________ **Date** __________

Directions: Trace the 2s on the first line. Write a row of 2s in the second line. Trace the word two on the third line. Practice writing the word two on the fourth line.

Two 2

2 2 2 2 2 2 2

two two two two two

Name ______________________ **Date** __________

Directions: Write the capital and small forms of the letter Ii. *Write the letter* i *under the picture whose name has the /ī/ sound.*

Ii

Ii

I

i

Name ____________________ **Date** ________

Three 3

Directions: Trace the 3s on the first line. Write a row of 3s in the second line. Trace the word *three* on the third line. Practice writing the word *three* on the fourth line.

3 3 3 3 3 3 3

three three three three

Name ______________________ **Date** __________

Directions: Write the letter i under each picture whose name has the /ī/ sound.

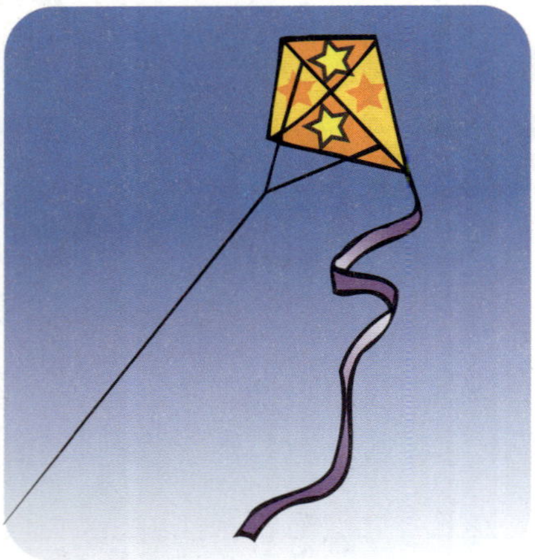

Name ______________________ Date ________

Directions: Listen carefully as I read each sentence. Circle the picture that matches the action in the sentence.

1. They are running.

2. He eats.

3. She walks.

4. He jumps rope.

5. She is reading.

Name ______________________ **Date** __________

Directions: Listen carefully as I read each sentence.

1. 

The cat plays with the yarn.

The cat played with the yarn.

2. 

They are kicking the ball.

They kicked the ball.

3. 

They are playing a game

They played a game.

4. 

He washes the car.

He washed the car.

Name ____________________ **Date** ________

2

3

Directions: Write the numbers 2 and 3 on the lines. Count the number of apples in each tree and write the correct number on the line.

UNIT 8

Lesson 10

Name ______________________________ **Date** __________

Directions: Listen carefully as I read each sentence. Circle the word in the sentence that shows action.

1. Michael eats a banana.

2. Carla mailed a letter.

3. The boy paints a picture.

4. They talk about school.

5. Dad and Zach fished on the dock.

6. Eric drives the car.

Name ______________________ **Date** ________

Directions: Trace the *4s* on the first line. Write a row of *4s* on the second line. Trace the word *four* on the third line. Practice writing the word *four* on the fourth line.

Four 4

4 4 4 4 4 4 4

four four four four four

Name ______________________ **Date** __________

Directions: Listen as I read each sentence. Look at the picture. Blend and read each word. Circle the best word to complete the sentence and then write the word on the line.

Kim sees boats on the ______________.

pen
lake

We see a ______________ in the ocean.

went
wave

Look at the clock.

What ______________ is it?

time
late

Name ______________________ Date __________

Directions: Look at each group of words carefully and listen as I read them. Circle the word or words that match the tense I read. Think about whether something has already happened, is happening now, or will happen later.

1. walked walk will walk

2. jump jumped will jump

3. wash washed will wash

4. clapped clap will clap

5. listen listened will listen

Name ______________________ Date ________

Directions: Listen carefully as I read each sentence. Circle the sentence that shows the action in the tense I say. Think about whether something has already happened, is happening now, or will happen later.

6. We listen to the teacher.
   We listened to the teacher.

7. He kicked the ball.
   He will kick the ball.

8. Mary will walk home from school.
   Mary walked home from school.

9. The dog fetches the newspaper.
   The dog will fetch the newspaper.

10. Louis spills milk.
    Louis spilled milk.

Name ______________________ **Date** ________

Five 5

5 5 5 5 5 5 5

five five five five five

Directions: Trace the 5s on the first line. Write a row of 5s on the second line. Trace the word *five* on the third line. Practice writing the word *five* on the fourth line.

Name ______________________ **Date** __________

Directions: Blend and read each word. Circle the best word to complete the sentence and then write the word on the line.

We played a ______________.

cane

game

Emma wins the ______________.

rule

race

He took a ______________.

pine

bite

Name ______________________ **Date** ________

Directions: Write the numbers *4* and *5* on the lines. Count the number of apples in each tree and write the correct number on the line.

4

5

Name ______________________ **Date** ________

Directions: Listen as I read each word that shows action. Draw a line from the word in the first column to the matching picture of the action in the second column.

1. swim

2. jump

3. drive

4. eat

5. read

Name ____________________ Date __________

Directions: Write the capital and small forms of the letter Oo. Write the letter o under the picture whose name has the /ō/ sound in it.

Oo

O o

O

o

Name ______________________ **Date** __________

six 6

Directions: Trace the 6s on the first line. Write a row of 6s on the second line. Trace the word *six* on the third line. Practice writing the word *six* on the fourth line.

6 6 6 6 6 6 6

six six six six six six

Name ______________________ **Date** __________

Directions: Write the letter *o* under each picture whose name begins with the /ō/ sound.

Name ______________________ **Date** __________

Directions: Listen carefully as I read the words that name. Circle the word that matches the category I say: *person, animal, thing,* or *place.*

1. cat book boy

2. wagon elephant teacher

3. car banana school

4. ball dog farmer

5. girl mouse apple

Name ______________________ Date __________

Directions: Write the letter *o* under each picture whose name has the /ō/ sound in the middle sound.

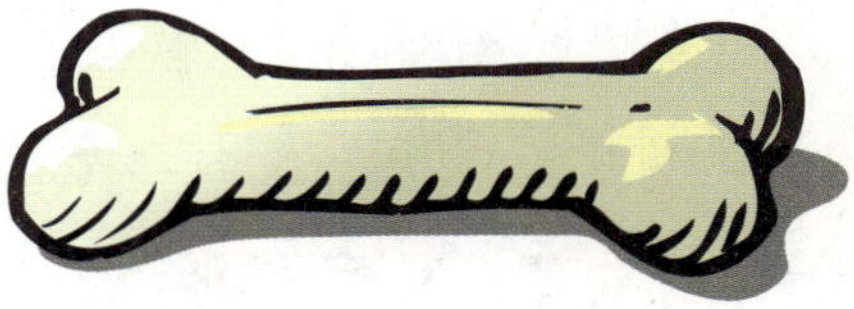

Name ______________________ **Date** __________

Directions: Trace the 7s on the first line. Write a row of 7s on the second line. Trace the word *seven* on the third line. Practice writing the word *seven* on the fourth line.

seven 7

7 7 7 7 7 7 7

seven seven seven

Name ______________________ **Date** ________

Directions: Write the letter *o* under each picture whose name has the /ō/ sound at the end.

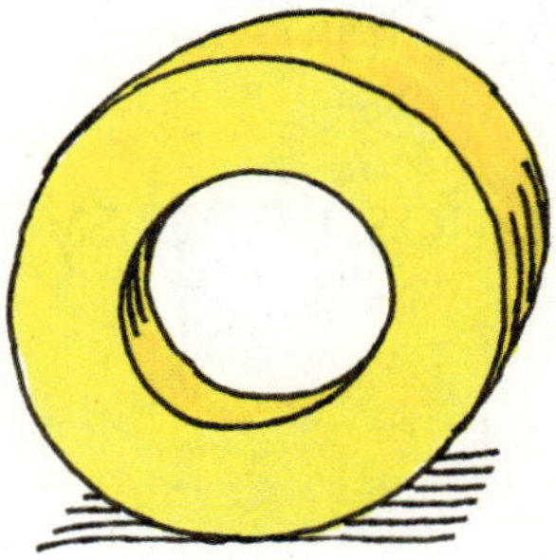

Name ______________________ **Date** ________

Directions: Listen carefully as I read each sentence. Circle the sentence that uses capital letters correctly.

1. Does Josh wear glasses?

   Yes, josh and sydney wear glasses.

2. Can anthony come out to play?

   No, Anthony is eating dinner now.

3. Is emma afraid of the Dog?

   No, Emma loves to play with dogs!

4. Will Matt sing the song for us?

   Yes, matt will sing the Song for us.

5. Does Madison like to swim?

   Yes, madison likes to swim.

Name ______________________ Date __________

Directions: Write the numbers 6 and 7 on the lines. Count the number of apples in each tree and write the correct number on the line.

6 ______________________

7 ______________________

______________ ______________

Name ______________________ **Date** __________

Directions: Write the capital and small forms of the letter *Uu*. Write the letter *u* under each picture whose name has the /ū/ sound in it.

Uu

Uu

U

u

Name ______________________ **Date** __________

Directions: Trace the 8s on the first line. Write a row of 8s on the second line. Trace the word *eight* on the third line. Practice writing the word *eight* on the fourth line.

eight 8

8 8 8 8 8 8 8

eight eight eight eight

Name ______________________ **Date** ________

Directions: Write the letter *u* under each picture whose name has the /ū/ sound in it.

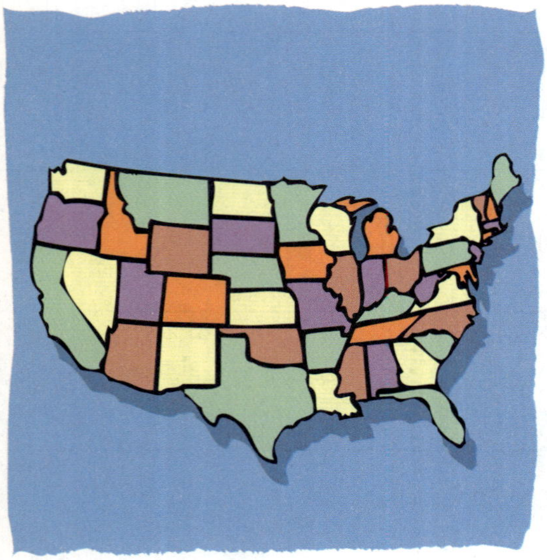

Name ______________________ **Date** __________

nine 9

Directions: Trace the 9s on the first line. Write a row of 9s on the second line. Trace the word *nine* on the third line. Practice writing the word *nine* on the fourth line.

9 9 9 9 9 9 9

nine nine nine nine

Name ______________________________ **Date** __________

Directions: Write the numbers 8 and 9 on the lines. Count the number of apples in each tree and write the correct number on the line.

8 ______________________________

9 ______________________________

______________ ______________

UNIT 9

Lesson 11

Name ______________________ **Date** __________

Directions: Write the letter *o* under each picture whose name has the /ō/ sound. Write the letter *u* under each picture whose name has the /ū/ sound.

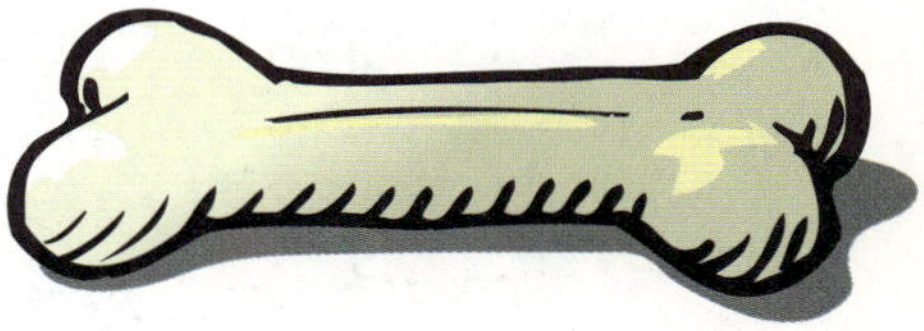

Name ______________________ Date __________

ten 10

Directions: Trace the *10*s on the first line. Write a row of *10*s on the second line. Trace the word *ten* on the third line. Practice writing the word *ten* on the fourth line.

10 10 10 10 10

ten ten ten ten ten ten

Name ______________________ **Date** __________

Directions: Look at each picture and count the apples. Write the number of apples on the line. Then write the name of the number.

0 zero	1 one	2 two
3 three	4 four	5 five

2 two

Name ____________________ **Date** __________

Directions: Listen as I read each sentence. Look at the picture. Blend and read each word. Circle the best word to fill the blank and then write the word on the line.

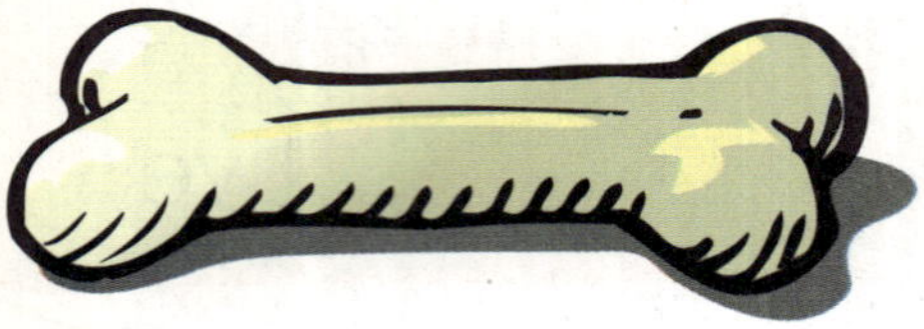

The dog likes to chew on a ____________. bone bake

The ____________ smells nice. hose rose

The ____________ pulled the cart. mule mail

Name ______________________ **Date** __________

Directions: Trace the capital letter at the beginning of each sentence. Add a period to sentences if needed.

1. The ball bounces.

2. School is fun

3. Cats play with yarn

4. Mice like cheese.

5. Eric points to the map

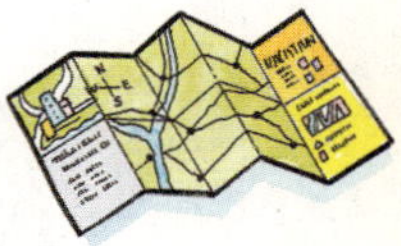

6. Fish have fins.

Name ______________________ Date ________

Directions: Look at each picture and count the apples. Write the number of apples on the line. Then write the name of the number.

6 six
7 seven
8 eight
9 nine
10 ten

10 ten

Name ____________________ Date __________

Directions: Write the capital and small forms of the letter *Ee*. Write the letter e under the picture whose name has the /ē/ sound in it.

Ee Ee

E

e

Name ______________________ Date ________

Directions: Write the letter e under each picture whose name has the /ē/ sound.

Name ____________________ **Date** __________

Directions: Write the letter *e* under the picture whose name begins with the /ē/ sound.

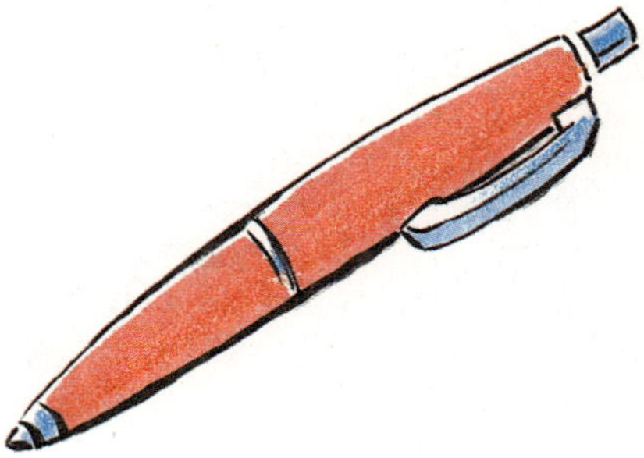

Name ______________________ **Date** ________

Directions: Listen as I read each sentence. Write the number of words in each sentence on the first line. Write the number of spaces in each sentence on the second line.

1. The eagle landed in the nest. ______ ______

2. Kate has a dog. ______ ______

3. We planted the seeds in the garden. ______ ______

4. They went to the beach. ______ ______

5. Nick went to the farm to see the turkey. ______ ______

6. Did you see that movie? ______ ______

Name ____________________ **Date** __________

Directions: Write the letter e under each picture whose name has the /ē/ sound in the middle sound.

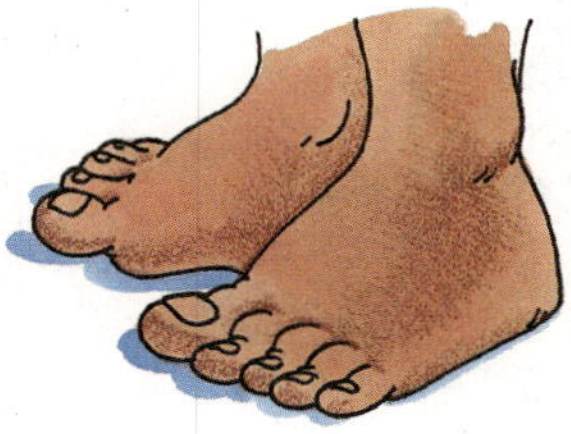

Name ______________________ **Date** __________

Directions: Write the letter e under each picture whose name ends with the /ē/ sound.

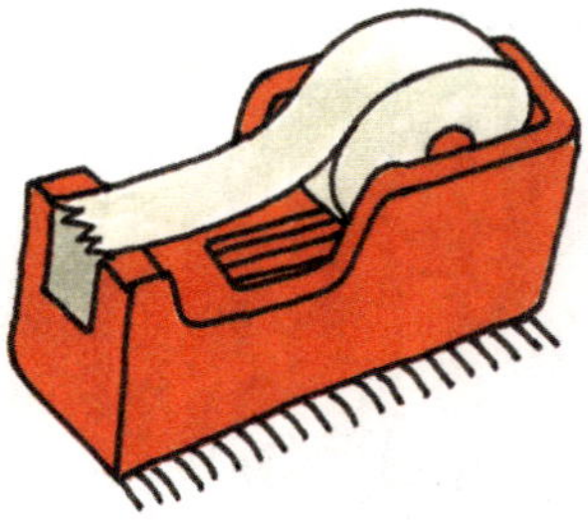

Name ______________________ Date ________

Directions: Listen carefully as I read each sentence. Write a period or question mark at the end of each sentence.

1. How are you ____

2. We scored a goal ____

3. Who caught the fish ____

4. Do you have a hat ____

5. The muffins are good ____

6. Where are the bananas ____

UNIT 10

Lesson 5

Name ______________________ **Date** __________

Directions: Listen as I read each sentence. Look at the picture. Blend and read each word. Circle the best word to fill the blank and then write the word on the line.

I. Sue wears a ____________.

cap cape

2. Is the ____________ in the shed?

rake wake

3. The ____________ looked at the dog.

bet vet

Name ______________________ Date __________

Directions: Write the capital *A* under each picture whose name has the /ā/ sound. Write a small *a* under each picture whose name has the /a/ sound.

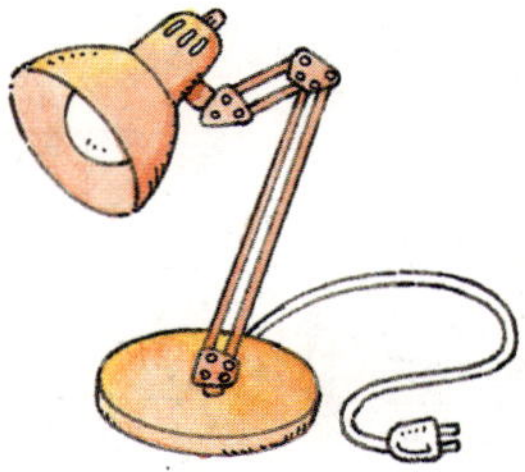

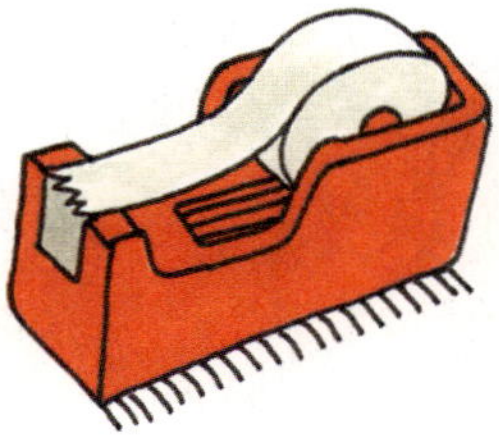

Name ______________________ **Date** __________

Directions: Listen as I read each sentence. Look at the picture. Blend and read each word. Circle the best word to fill the blank and then write the word on the line.

1. Look at the frog ____________.

hop hip

2. He is on the ____________.

sled sack

3. Pat can see the ____________.

bug beg

Name ____________________ Date ________

Directions: Listen as I read each sentence. Circle *yes* if the sentence is written correctly. Circle *no* if the sentence is not written correctly.

1. the person is painting.

yes no

2. We like to fish.

yes no

3. Are you going to school?

yes no

4. The butterfly is on the flower

yes no

5. Hurry or we will be late!

yes no

Name ______________________________ **Date** __________

Directions: Listen as I read each sentence and give the directions. Circle the correct answer.

6. The red apple is sweet.
Do you like red apples?

7. Where is the basket?
The basket is on the table.

8. I see a skunk by the tree.
Be careful!

9. The airplane flew by
. ? !

10. Could you see the pilot
. ? !

Name ______________________ **Date** __________

Directions: Listen as I read each sentence. Blend and read each word. Then write the word that completes each sentence.

Can you hear the ____________? buzz fuzz

Frankie the ____________ is friendly. box fox

The apple juice is in the ____________. jog jug

Name ______________________ **Date** ________

Directions: Listen as I read each sentence. Blend and read each word. Then write the word that completes each sentence.

Dan's ball is on the ____________.   rug   bug

Do you like corn on the ____________?   cob   bog

Spin the ____________!   mop   top

Name ______________________ **Date** ________

Directions: Listen as I read each sentence. Look at the picture. Blend and read each word. Circle the best word to fill the blank and then write the word on the line.

1. This is my ______________.

cat bike

2. We want to sit by the ______________.

lake bike

3. The ______________ are in the pond.

socks ducks

Name ______________________ **Date** __________

Directions: Listen as I read each sentence. Look at the picture. Circle the correct position word to fill the blank and then write the word on the line.

1. The ball is ____________ the box.

on in

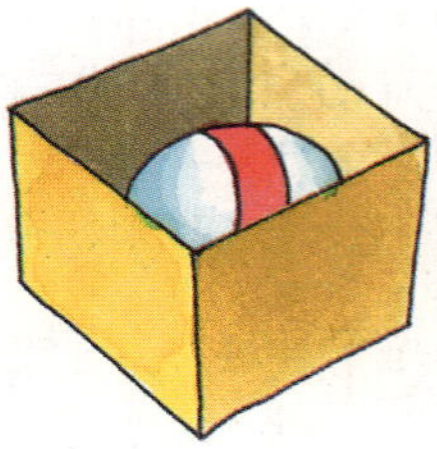

2. The chicken is ____________ the duck.

beside over

3. The cat is ____________ the bowls.

under between

Name ______________________ **Date** __________

Directions: Listen as I read each sentence. Blend and read each word. Then write the word that completes each sentence.

We have a big ____________.

trip

van

She plays with the ____________.

wag

yo-yo

The ____________ wears a crown.

queen

quit

Name ________________________ Date __________

Directions: Listen as I read each sentence. Blend and read each word. Then write the word that completes each sentence.

The baby is in the ______________. crib bib

Stan likes to drink ______________. milk silk

Mike has a ______________. nap cap

Name ______________________ Date ________

Directions: Listen as I read each sentence and the answers. Circle the pronoun that replaces the underlined word or words.

1. Marty and I have a dog.

They He We

2. The ball is yellow.

It He She

3. Anita likes school.

We She It

4. Mr. Lopez is the teacher.

They He She

5. Charlie and Mike are friends.

He We They

6. Are my sister and I late?

you we they

Name ______________________ **Date** ________

Directions: Listen as I read each sentence and the answers. Circle the word or words that replaces the underlined pronoun.

7. <u>It</u> is black.

The sun The ant

8. <u>I</u> was there.

Jamie and Mary Jamie

9. <u>She</u> jumps.

Kate Henry

10. <u>They</u> run.

David and Tom Tom and I

11. <u>We</u> eat.

Jane and I Jane and Sue

12. <u>He</u> drives.

Anita Mark

Name ______________________ **Date** ________

Directions: Listen as I read each sentence. Blend and read each word. Then write the word that completes each sentence.

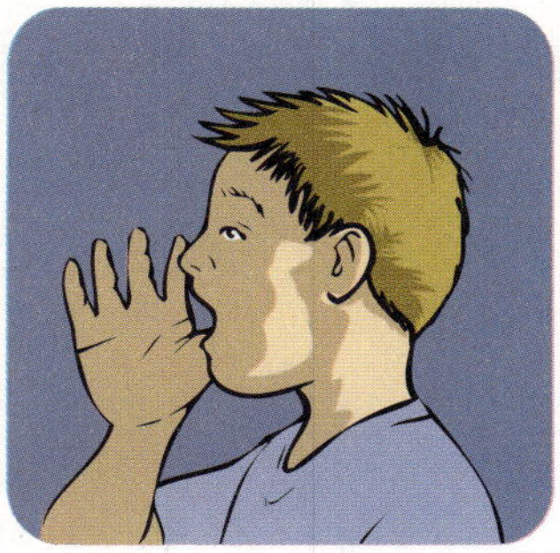

Please do not ______________.

well
yell

He wears a ______________.

vest
yes

There is a ______________ today.

kiss
test

Name ______________________ Date ________

Directions: Listen as I read each sentence. Blend and read each word. Then write the word that completes each sentence.

We learned about a great ____________. ring king

A big ____________ came onto the beach. vase wave

Lili's ____________ won the game. kick tick